# A M E R I C A N
# CASTLES

## — A Pictorial History —

### Amy Handy

# TODTRI

This book was designed and published by
TODTRI Book Publishers
254 West 31st Street, New York, NY 10001-2813
Fax: (212) 695-6984
E-mail: info@todtri.com

*Visit us on the web!*
*www.todtri.com*

Library of Congress Cataloging-in-Publication
Number 97-66814

ISBN 1-57717-068-7

*Author:* Amy Handy

*Publisher:* Robert M. Tod
*Editorial Director:* Elizabeth Loonan
*Book Designer:* Mark Weinberg
*Senior Editor:* Cynthia Sternau
*Project Editor:* Ann Kirby
*Photo Editors:* Edward Douglas, Laura Wyss
*Typesetting:* Command-O Design

*Printed and bound in Singapore*

# PICTURE CREDITS

**Belcourt Castle, Newport, Rhode Island**
Keith Henry 16, 18
Jim McElholm 17

**The Biltmore Estate, Asheville, North Carolina** 52 (top), 53

**BOB-E Photographs**
Robert R. Edwards 78

**Woodfin Camp & Associates**
Bernard Boutrit 39

**Comstock, Inc.**
Gary J. Benson 15
Wingstock 66 (bottom), 74

**Corbis-Bettmann**
5, 6, 7, 29, 30 (left), 62 (bottom), 66 (top)

**Eric Crossan** 13

**David Davis Mansion, Bloomington, Illinois** 58 (top & bottom), 59

**John Elk III** 20, 23, 24–25, 26, 27, 60, 61, 77

**FPG International**
Richard Laird 45
Kit Latham 30–31, 49

**Erika Klass** 68 (top & bottom)

**James M. Majuto** 12

**Patti McConville** 14

**Steve Melzer** 67

**Larry Mulvehill** 4, 10

**New England Stock Photo**
Jean Higgins 51
Thomas H. Mitchell 11
Jim Schwabel 19, 40–41, 42
Clyde H. Smith 65
John Wells 55

**Omni-Photo Communications**
Grace Davies 76
Jeff Greenberg 69

**Photophile**
Mark Gibson 28
Sal Maimone 56–57
L.L.T. Rhodes 62 (top), 63

**The Picture Cube**
Walter Bibikow 46, 50, 52 (bottom)
Francie Manning 36
Todd Phillips 64

**Picture Perfect**
Donna Bryant 54 (top)
Dave & Les Jacobs 72–73
Allan Montaine 35

**The Preservation Society of Newport County**
8–9, 32, 33, 34, 37, 38, 43, 44, 47, 48

**Ann Purcell** 22

**Carl Purcell** 21, 75

**H. Armstrong Roberts**
W. Bertsch 79
J. Blank 70

**Carol Simowitz** 54 (bottom)

**Lee Snider** 71 (top & bottom)

# CONTENTS

# THE GILDED AGE

**A**merica was established as a nation without royalty, founded by pioneers unbound by the strict social stratification that gave rise to the great monarchies of Europe. Yet as fortunes were won in the New World, a new aristocracy arose, one determined not so much by birthright as by basic economics. And those industrious, smart, ruthless, or merely lucky enough to find themselves in possession of great wealth sought to create homes as lavish and beautiful as those of the crowned heads of Europe.

## A HISTORY OF THE GILDED AGE

*From post–Civil War reconstruction until the Stock Market crash of 1929, America experienced a period of almost inconceivable economic growth. Dubbed "The Gilded Age" by Mark Twain, it was also a time of exploitative profiteering, with a small group of Americans benefiting from the growth of the nation's industrial base, often at the cost of the lives of laborers, especially the nation's newly arriving immigrants.*

*Charles Darwin had published his theory of evolution in* The Origin of Species *in 1859; consequently a new concept of social Darwinism began to take hold of the American intellect, fostering a belief in the survival of the fittest in human society as well as in nature. Though this rationale was often used to defend the fortunes of the day, in truth most of this great wealth was accumulated not by healthy competition but by creation of huge monopolies known as trusts.*

*From the 1890s on, a new progressive attitude among the working class beat at the foundations of the old monopolies. Progressive journalists, known as "the muckrakers," exposed the ruthless, unfair, and often illegal methods of the trusts. The captains of industry became known as the*

*LEFT:* **The portico of Frederick Vanderbilt's Hyde Park mansion offers a breathtaking view of the Hudson River and the surrounding valley.** *Hyde Park, New York*

*ABOVE:* **Mrs. Alva Smith Vanderbilt presided over Marble House in Newport, Rhode Island for four years, until she remarried and moved across the avenue. After her second husband died twelve years later, she opened Marble House to the public to raise money for the women's suffrage movement.**

"robber barons," and by the turn of the century anti-trust legislation was bringing an end to the monopolies of the Gilded Age.

Yet the great fortunes remained, and with uncontrolled speculation on Wall Street and continued growth of the nation and its economy, they continued to grow and be spent in high style. Families like the Hearsts, the Vanderbilts, and the Rockefellers, established before the turn of the century, quickly became the American equivalent of royalty, wealthy and powerful beyond belief.

## IMPORTING HISTORY

In order to begin a noble tradition from which others in the New World could aspire, this new class of wealthy Americans sought to establish a self-made royal status.

The arrival of ocean liners and the railroad enabled America's upper class to travel extensively and in great luxury. Exposed to the historic castles of Europe, they spent lavishly to create a world within the American society that emulated the ways of the Old World, and built fantastic and opulent homes in the tradition of European nobility—symbols of their status, wealth, and refinement. They copied the

*ABOVE:* In typical Victorian style, the art gallery of Lyndhurst was thoroughly crammed with paintings, hung floor to ceiling with almost no space in between. *Tarrytown, New York*

ancient architectural styles, seeking to give their homes a history that tied them more closely to the classical civilizations of old. As America's new upper class struggled to find meaning and context for their good fortune, the architects of the day presented them with a variety of options with which to express their wealth.

Culturally, they saw themselves as heirs to a great western tradition of art and culture, collecting artifacts from ancient Greece and Rome and Medieval and Renaissance Europe. With ample financial resources and an inclination toward exploitation of resources, they bought and disassembled great works of art, rooms, even entire buildings, and had them shipped home to be reassembled on their American estates.

In a land devoid of ancient castles and fortresses, the American aristocracy of the Gilded Age built pleasure palaces that sometimes exceeded even the highest of expectations. Craftsmen and artisans from around the world brought the flavors and techniques of many cultures together, reviving classic architectural styles and generating new ones. Some homes strictly adhered to a particular period style; at Lyndhurst, for example, both the architecture and the furnishings reflect a purely Gothic style. Other estates, such as William Randolph Hearst's Enchanted Hill, show a unique blend of architectural styles, with antique furnishings and artworks eclectically assembled. Still others, such as Whitehall, utilized antiques and architectural details to create period rooms dedicated to different eras and styles.

The castles of the United States show a commitment to the stately homes of old as well as a brash sense of individuality that typifies the American spirit. Unchained to any particular style, the elite of the Gilded Age drew liberally from a variety of eras and regions when designing their homes, blending their influences carefully to reflect and enhance the priceless works of arts with which they filled them.

## AMERICAN ROYALTY

The story of the American castle is more than a survey of eclectic architectural styles. The first families of American society built homes that suited their own styles, their own needs, and their own personal histories. American royalty was royalty without birthright, and those who rose up to the top of the socio-economic ladder in a land founded on the notion that all men are created equal often felt it was their duty to give back to the nation that which they had taken. Their need to do good works—often in harsh juxtaposition with their sometimes ruthless business practices—sprung not only from the progressive mood of the early 1900s, but also from a desire to tie themselves socially to the wealthy classes of Europe.

Spiritually, they emulated the moneyed classes of Renaissance Italy, the great patrons of the arts who collected the world's treasures, supported artists, and felt a strong sense of moral obligation to public service. They championed worthy causes and helped those in need. Their homes, in many cases, were built with the intention of eventually becoming museums, and, indeed, many of the stately homes of the Gilded Age are today open to the public as cultural and artistic landmarks.

The Gilded Age represents a unique time in American history, encompassing the evolution of the society from the proper Victorian attitudes of the mid-nineteenth century to the devil-may-care mood of the roaring 1920s. While a great many stately homes were built

before and after the Gilded Age, those built between the Civil War and the Great Depression tell a singular story, and capture a special part of American culture in its infancy. They define the birth of a new social class, and reflect the growth of a nation in a time of sweeping changes. These palaces were the homes not of kings and queens but of businessmen who had made fortunes in the land that was supposed to hold enough wealth for everyone, and came to represent the basic American belief that anything is possible given equal and ample opportunity and determination.

*ABOVE:* Hearst entertains dinner guests in a hall constructed from the interior of a Spanish church. Many of the host's guests were international celebrities. The woman in the foreground with her back to the camera is Marion Davies, the actress who became Hearst's constant companion.

RIGHT: Soaring to a height of 45 feet, the Great Hall of The Breakers affords a suitably grand entrance to the palatial seventy-room home. *Newport, Rhode Island*

# CHAPTER ONE

# GOTHIC CASTLES

In a young nation not far removed from its European ancestry, the castle remained the epitome of lavish living. But while the great castles of Europe date back hundreds, even thousands of years, the most notable of American fortunes were won no earlier than the mid-nineteenth century. Wealthy Americans would seek to create an architectural history as opulent as Europe's on American soil.

The great castles and cathedrals of Europe are some of the most beautiful buildings ever constructed, reflecting the Gothic notion of architecture as high art. Details such as stone tracery filled with stained glass, high vaulted ceilings, flying buttresses, and elaborate decoration—hallmarks of Gothic design—inspired many wealthy Americans as they traveled through Europe in the mid-nineteenth century.

A great Gothic revival swept through the west just as new fortunes were being earned and spent by the great industrialists of the era. Coupled with the Arts and Crafts movement led by William Morris and others, the Gothic revival influenced the building and interior designs for some of the most elegant and imposing homes erected during the Gilded Age.

The castles of America draw on a variety of influences, some remaining true to the Gothic model, while others mix medieval elements with those of the Baroque and Renaissance styles. Many were built as self-sufficient estates, with their own gardens and farming operations; others are smaller in scale but no less impressive.

## THE AMERICAN GOTHIC CASTLE

Of all the styles influencing the great homes of the Gilded Age, the Gothic is among the most pervasive and certainly the most distinctive. Inspired by the cathedrals of medieval Europe and fueled by a revival in the Gothic arts spearheaded by the Pre-Raphaelite brotherhood in mid-nineteenth century England, architects of the New World set about creating castles so true to the Gothic form that they seem to have been

*BELOW:* Inventor John Hays Hammond began constructing his medieval-style masonry castle in 1925 as a home and museum dedicated to the arts and sciences. *Gloucester, Massachusetts*

plucked from a European landscape painting and placed down on a fresh plot of land in America.

Often, this was not far from the truth. When constructing his *Abbadia Mare*, "Abbey by the Sea," inventor John Hays Hammond incorporated actual portions of medieval dwellings, and reproduced countless others. More commonly known as Hammond Castle, the masonry castle towers above the rocky coast near Gloucester, Massachusetts, and features such Gothic hallmarks as turrets, battlements, flying buttresses, and a

*LEFT:* Set against the blazing colors of autumn, Osborn Castle seems to float above the Hudson Valley. Built in the nineteenth century, the house, unlike many of its kind, is still privately owned. *Garrison, New York*

drawbridge. Construction began in 1925 on the castle, which was built from Hammond's own plans and dedicated to the arts and sciences. Hammond conceived the structure not merely as a stately home, but as a museum dedicated to the arts and sciences. An inventor holding nearly one thousand individual patents, Hammond was an electronics pioneer, responsible for countless innovations in the realms of electronics and national defense. He was also an avid collector of antiquities, procuring countless antiques and architectural details—including fireplaces, art-

works, and tiles—with which to furnish the castle.

Hammond's Great Hall captures the essence of Gothic beauty, designed in the spirit and scale of an authentic medieval cathedral. Featuring a large stained-glass window patterned after the rose window at the ancient Rheims Cathedral in France, the stone Great Hall is over 100 feet long and features a fantastic, 65-foot-high ceiling spanned by wooden arches. The spectacular pipe organ—which took Hammond some twenty years to built—sits in an 85-foot-high stone tower that opens into the Great Hall.

*ABOVE:* Hammond Castle incorporates furnishings and architectural portions from buildings of the Roman, medieval, and Renaissance periods. The tower was designed to accommodate the castle's celebrated pipe organ. *Gloucester, Massachusetts*

*RIGHT:* Nemours Mansion, designed by Carrère and Hastings for industrialist Alfred I. du Pont in 1909, was filled with the latest domestic technology, including an ice-making room and a water-bottling machine. The estate's formal French gardens are reminiscent of those at Versailles. *Wilmington, Delaware*

*RIGHT:* **Perched on a hilltop above the Hudson River, Lyndhurst is one of the country's finest Gothic revival mansions.** *Tarrytown, New York*

No less impressive is Lyndhurst Castle, the premiere example of Gothic revival architecture in the United States, located alongside the Hudson River in Tarrytown, New York. While many of the great mansions of America bear the mark of a singular person or family, Lyndhurst Castle has passed through three families and several generations, creating a history more in line with that of the great castles of Europe. Yet despite the changing hands of ownership and major expansion of the original structure, the style of the thirty-room castle and its furnishings remains true to the Gothic revival form.

Built in 1838 for General William Paulding and his son Philip, who was mayor of New York City from 1824–26, the castle known now as Lyndhurst was at the time called by a variety of names, including Paulding's Villa, Paulding's Manor, The Knoll, and, by their political opposition, Paulding's Folly. Renowned architect Alexander Jackson Davis designed the original structure, which included two main floors as well as a basement and attic, and boasted such elaborate architectural details as towers, turrets, buttresses, and pinnacled roofs. The second floor was divided into extravagant chambers, including Paulding's library, and the first floor included a large drawing and dining room. Beautiful windows, parquetry floors, and detailed ceilings of rib vaulting or haunched beams decorate the interior.

In 1864 the estate was sold to New York dry goods merchant George Merrit, who renamed the estate Lyndhurst. Under Merrit's direction, the building was nearly doubled in size, with a new

*ABOVE:* **The thirty-room stone-and-marble main building of Lyndhurst boasts all the trappings of the Gothic style, including turrets, buttresses, and pinnacled roofs.**
*Tarrytown, New York*

north wing and a tower joining the old and new portions. Fortunately, the architectural style was maintained throughout the renovations, and the result was a uniformly executed castle in the Gothic revival style. Merrit also developed the grounds, draining the swampy land and creating some twenty acres of lawns, trees, and shrubs. Fruit trees and vegetable gardens were planted, as well as a formidable grape arbor.

In the 1870s, Lyndhurst was sold to Jay Gould, a notorious robber baron who had made his fortune in railroad securities, allegedly profiting from such shady business practices as stock manipulation, creating rumors and false panics, and bribery. The son of a poor farmer, Gould

went to work early in his life and by the age of twenty-one had saved $5,000, which he began investing in the leather business and railroad stocks. Ten years later, he was a director of the Erie Railroad, soon after waging a vicious war with Cornelius Vanderbilt for control of the system. At the peak of his career in 1881, he owned more railroad mileage than any other individual or group in the nation.

However, his personal life acted in sharp juxtaposition to his unscrupulous business style. He is said to have been a loving family man, and posthumous revelations uncovered a number of philanthropic endeavors Gould had performed anonymously. Gould and his family lived at

*BELOW:* **Belcourt's master bedroom houses the Maharajah of Jaipur's bed, crafted from magnificently carved teakwood.** *Newport, Rhode Island*

Lyndhurst for two generations, and made few alterations to the structure other than adding modern conveniences such as small electric lighting and additional plumbing. After Gould's death, his daughters maintained the house and grounds with little change to its original architecture. Repairs were executed in exact duplication of the original, and furnishings remained faithful to the Gothic style. Today, the castle is opened to the public for tours and events.

Less dedicated to one particular style is Belcourt Castle, the Newport, Rhode Island, mansion of Oliver Hazard Perry Belmont. Designed by Richard Morris Hunt, the Louis XIII-style hunting lodge included a single bedroom in the medieval style and quarters for a large staff of servants. Coaches entered through the ground floor, where a large stable offered generous accommodations for thirty horses. In 1896 Belmont married Alva Smith Vanderbilt, ex-wife of William K. Vanderbilt and the owner of the most lavish home in Newport, Marble House, which the Vanderbilts had built during their marriage. However, she chose to stay at Belcourt with her new husband, and kept Marble House closed. After Oliver's death in 1908, Alva renovated Belcourt to accommodate motor cars, which were then gradually replacing the horse and carriage as the preferred means of transportation.

*BELOW:* **Oliver Belmont wanted his horses housed in the same grandeur to which he himself was accustomed. Much of Belcourt's ground floor was thus constructed as an enormous stable. Each horse received bedding of pure Irish linen embroidered with the Belmont crest.** *Newport, Rhode Island*

*ABOVE:* The English Library at Belcourt is paneled with oak carved in Gothic-style linenfold. The elegantly sculpted fireplace is finished in scagliola, a high-quality imitation of ornamental marble. *Newport, Rhode Island*

*RIGHT:* Conceived in the style of the Louis XIII hunting lodge at Versailles, Belcourt Castle was commissioned by Oliver Hazard Perry Belmont and designed by Richard Morris Hunt. *Newport, Rhode Island*

## THE MOST FAMOUS CASTLE IN AMERICA

Publishing magnate William Randolph Hearst (1863–1951) took a spread of family-owned land in the hills near San Francisco and turned it into *La Cuesta Encantada*, "The Enchanted Hill." More commonly known as Hearst Castle, this palatial 125-acre estate in San Simeon, California, combines the Spanish Renaissance style of architecture with a wealth of priceless artifacts retrieved from ancient monasteries and archaeological sites throughout Europe. Hearst's fascinating life, career, and personality are reflected in every room, furnishing, and detail in what is said to be the most costly private home ever constructed in the United States.

The son of a wealthy mining tycoon, William Randolph Hearst began life with a tidy fortune and aspirations of becoming a newspaperman. His father, George Hearst, had acquired the *San Francisco Examiner* in 1880 as payment of a gambling debt, and turned the paper over to William seven years later. The younger Hearst took after the world of journalism with a passion, acquiring *The New York Journal* in 1895 and inciting a heated circulation war with Joseph Pulitzer's *New York*

*LEFT:* La Casa Grande ("the great house") forms the main building of Hearst Castle, the cost of which, over its thirty years of construction, was reputed to be $20 million. *San Simeon, California*

*ABOVE:* La Casa Del Sol, a guest cottage on the grounds of Hearst Castle. Set on the warm coast of southern California, Hearst Castle is surrounded by dense greenery and towering palm trees. *San Simeon, California*

*World*, a newspaper at which he had worked only a few years prior.

As a journalist and entrepreneur, Hearst was both ruthless and visionary. He not only built a newspaper chain that continues to thrive today but also broke ground in the film industry, producing countless newsreels, movie serials, and more than one hundred films, becoming perhaps the first mogul of the multi-media age. Interestingly, much of Hearst's celebrity came from his newspaper's decidedly progressive stance. The paper served as a platform for his personal opinion, and he frequently condemned the immoral and inhumane ways of the wealthy robber barons, to the approval naturally of his working-class readership.

Hearst's fortune grew, and his grandiose lifestyle among society's jet set earned him an almost mythic reputation. His life and career inspired Orson Welles's film masterpiece, *Citizen Kane*, regarded by movie buffs and critics the world over as perhaps the finest film ever made. The movie opens with spectacular views of Xanadu, the fictional home of Welles's protagonist, Charles Foster Kane. Stocked with priceless pieces of art, opulent and outrageous rooms, and even a private zoo, Xanadu is spectacular; it is, however, a shadow of the actual Hearst castle that inspired it.

The property itself was originally a 40,000-acre ranch, purchased by Hearst's father in 1865; he later expanded the property to 240,000 acres. The Hearsts held informal parties at an elevated campsite on the property, developing their own, majestic definition of "camping on the hill." By the time William inherited the property in 1919, the campground consisted of a luxurious tent village, complete with a dining hall, social hall, and sleeping quarters.

Hearst, who had been living with his wife in New York, decided to set up his headquarters at San Simeon. In 1919 he approached architect Julia Morgan—a civil engineer from the University of California at Berkeley and the first woman to receive a certificate in architecture from the Ecole des Beaux-Arts in Paris—to design a permanent dwelling on the property, "something that would be more comfortable" than the platform tents that were used on the ranch. Construction on the estate began in 1919 and continued until 1947.

Building commenced with the construction of three guest cottages, each named for its outstanding views and consisting of up to eighteen rooms: La Casa Del Monte faces the Santa Lucia Mountains; La Casa Del Sol faces the setting sun; and La Casa Del Mar offers a stunning view of the sea. Construction of La Casa Grande, the great house, began before the last of the cottages was complete.

The estate is designed in the Spanish Renaissance style, with red-tiled roofs, white marble latticework, and elaborate copper domes. Hearst avidly collected priceless artworks and antiquities, and called for constant revisions in the building plan to accommodate his newest acquisitions. He dismantled and imported furnishings and rooms from ancient ruins, among them a mosaic floor dating from the first century A.D. which was brought from Pompeii and installed in the spacious entry vestibule. In the grand assembly hall, an intricately carved ceiling was also brought from Italy and installed two stories above without any alterations. Two ancient marble medallions,

*BELOW:* **Beautiful sculptures and other art objects, collected from around the world, adorn the grounds of Hearst Castle.** *San Simeon, California*

FOLLOWING PAGE: Hearst Castle's outdoor Neptune pool, built entirely of marble, is flanked by marble colonnades and a temple façade housing a sculptured figure of the sea god Neptune on its pediment. *San Simeon, California*

LEFT: The Doge's suite of Hearst Castle features, in appropriately Venetian style, an ornately carved ceiling and fireplace and richly upholstered walls. *San Simeon, California*

carved in Denmark and each weighing close to a ton, adorn the assembly room walls, and seventeenth-century Flemish tapestries hang above ornately carved wood choir stalls which were retrieved from an old Italian monastery.

Hearst's favorite room is said to have been the refectory, a grand dining hall featuring a dark wood ceiling carved with reliefs of the saints, brought from an Italian monastery. Beautifully detailed tapestries depicting the life of the prophet Daniel line the side walls, while an old Gothic mantle from a French château marks one end of the room.

The outdoor Neptune pool is constructed entirely of marble with a distinctive geometric design laid into the patterned floor. It is surrounded by classical sculptures, and a flanked by a Grecian-Roman temple façade, which houses a sculpture of the god Neptune. Hearst demanded that the water in the 345,000-gallon pool be kept at a uniform seventy degrees.

Even more lavish is the indoor Roman pool, located in the rear of the main house. The last structure to be completed on the estate, it is large enough to comfortably accommodate the two tennis courts that sit on its roof. The pool itself as well as the surrounding walls are covered in magnificent mosaics, executed by a crew of Italian artisans who laid thousands of tiny Venetian tiles over four years, at an estimated cost of a million dollars.

Hearst—and Hearst Castle—lived the high life from the roaring twenties through World War II. In his later years, Hearst's constant companion at the palace was Miss Marion Davies, a Ziegfeld Follies showgirl less than half his age. While their romance instigated much gossip, their parties at the celebrated castle hosted such guests as Winston Churchill, George Bernard Shaw, Carole Lombarde, Charlie Chaplin, Errol Flynn, and Buster Keaton.

Hearst sold 140,000 acres of the estate to the United States government at the outbreak of World War II as a training ground for troops, and remained there until he became ill in 1946 and was advised by doctors to relocate to a less isolated spot. He died in 1951, and the estate was given to the people of California in his memory. As Hearst had desired, San Simeon was opened to the public in 1958 as a center for the advancement of art and culture.

*LEFT:* **Hearst frequently used the Gothic study as part of his private suite. The arches contain highly detailed paintings of various figures and scenes.** *San Simeon, California*

*RIGHT:* **The refectory of Hearst Castle was said to be the owner's favorite room. The spectacular four-hundred-year-old wooden ceiling came from an Italian monastery.** *San Simeon, California*

# CHAPTER TWO

# VICTORIAN MANSIONS

**N**ot all the stately homes in America were designed to emulate the great Gothic castles of Europe. Many of the pleasure palaces of the United States were constructed in the Victorian mode, modeled after fine English manor homes and reflecting contemporary standards of propriety and decorum.

The Victorian style in itself is defined by eclecticism, borrowing from various eras and regional styles; Victorian style in fact is largely responsible for stylistic revivals such as the Gothic revival. Traditional and classic styles of architecture and design were executed using modern materials and machinery to meet the demands of Victorian households and, as such, the style was fairly common.

The formality of the Victorian home extended far beyond the architecture and furnishings. The great Victorian mansions of the Gilded Age reflect not only the aesthetic ideals of the era but also the rules of social etiquette.

*LEFT:* Mrs. Stuyvesant Fish attends a summer function with Miss Lata Robinson. Renowned for the vicious wit with which she poked fun at Newport's strict etiquette, Mrs. Fish hosted somewhat unconventional dinners at her mansion, Crossways, where the unusual mix of guests enjoyed a less stuffy evening than the typical high-society gathering.

*LEFT:* A unique example of American Carpenter's Gothic, the Wedding Cake House began as a plain yellow Georgian home. Legend holds that shipbuilder George Bourne surprised his fiancée by pretending they would live in the antiquated brick cottage, but when the newlyweds arrived the bride was pleasantly surprised to find their home covered in Victorian gingerbread. An alternative, perhaps even more romantic tale has it that Bourne had to return to sea before he even had time to eat his wedding cake, and that he himself created the intricate carvings by hand during many lonely hours aboard ship. *Kennebunk, Maine*

## THE MANSIONS OF NEWPORT

Newport, Rhode Island, was in many respects the center of high society during the Gilded Age. Already well known as a resort, Newport had been the summer residence of choice for wealthy Americans since the colonial era. By the mid-nineteenth century, a Newport "cottage" was an essential property for the upper crust of American society. It was nearer to the turn of the century, however, that the most opulent mansions were erected, still called cottages but built on a grand scale primarily for the purpose of lavish entertaining.

The mansions of Newport attest to the diversity of influences as well as the vast amount of money being spent on architectural endeavors during the

*ABOVE:* Miss Roberta Willard and Miss Betty Pierson dance at a Newport garden fête in the summer of 1915. Many such events raised money for charity; the proceeds for this one went to aid two causes, Belgian orphans and the Women's Congressional Union.

era. Beginning with the construction of several large, late-Gothic stone houses, the age of opulence quickly took over Newport, and large estates designed by such noted architects as Stanford White and William Morris Hunt began to eclipse one another one by one.

Inspiration for the great mansions of Newport came from far and wide. The Elms, summer residence of coal magnate Julius Berwind, was designed by little-known Philadelphia architect Horace Trumbauer, and modeled after the eighteenth-century Château d'Asnieres in France. Berwind was a self-made man who, coming from

*RIGHT:* Adapted from the eighteenth-century Château d'Asnieres near Paris (designed by the chief architect of Versailles), The Elms was built for coal magnate Julius Berwind as a summer residence for entertaining. *Newport, Rhode Island*

modest means, became the one of the nation's largest suppliers of coal; he saw a bit of himself in Trumbauer, an independent architect who had started at sixteen as an office boy at one of Philadelphia's leading architectural firms and was in business for himself eight years later. Before being commissioned for The Elms, Trumbauer had designed several elaborate residences in the Philadelphia area, including Grey Towers, which was one of the largest homes in the country at that time.

The Elms plan included three identical entrances, a feature that the Berwinds had admired at Buckingham Palace, and, inside, a grand marble staircase. However, some of the most distinctive features of The Elms are ones that might go unnoticed. For example, the entire mansion is heated with an intricate system powered by coal that Berwind had delivered via a specially-built underground railroad. And while the estate lacked an ocean view, the grounds offer some of the most extravagant landscaping in Newport.

*LEFT:* Perhaps to offset the absence of an ocean view, The Elms was given carefully landscaped grounds, complete with statue groups, sunken gardens, gazebos, and fountains, such as this one known as the Fountain of the Turtles. *Newport, Rhode Island*

*ABOVE:* The elaborate architecture of The Elms serves as an appropriately grand backdrop to an impressive art collection that includes European decorative arts and eighteenth-century Venetian paintings. The mansion's magnificent staircase is constructed of white marble edged with an intricate railing of wrought iron and bronze. *Newport, Rhode Island*

*RIGHT:* Primarily meant for lavish entertaining, Rosecliff features an entrance hall dominated by a heart-shaped staircase adorned with intricate plasterwork. *Newport, Rhode Island*

*RIGHT:* Renowned architect Stanford White modeled Rosecliff after the seventeenth-century Grand Trianon of Versailles. Rosecliff is the most classical-looking of the Newport mansions. *Newport, Rhode Island*

The ocean view played an important role in the design of Rosecliff, the Newport home of Theresa Fair Oelrichs, modeled after the Grand Trianon at Versailles, France, by renowned architect Stanford White. The daughter of an Irish immigrant who had made his fortune in the Gold Rush of 1849 and followed up by striking silver in Nevada ten years later, Theresa Fair married prominent New York society man Hermann Oelrichs, thus solidifying her position in society with the all-important combination of wealth and name. She and her sister, Virginia Fair, purchased the Rosecliff estate and hired the architectural firm of McKim, Mead and White to design her summer palace.

Designed for grand-scale entertaining, Rosecliff features the largest ballroom in Newport, which takes up most of the ground floor. Here, Mrs. Oelrichs hosted some of the most glamorous balls in the city, the most celebrated of which was the *Bal Blanc*, or White Ball, a celebration of the Astor Cup race. For the occasion Mrs. Oelrichs transformed Rosecliff into a world of white, with white flowers throughout and ladies with powdered hair dressed entirely in white. When her request to "borrow" a few of the Navy's "White Fleet" ships was denied, Mrs. Oelrichs arranged for a dozen full-sized artificial white ships to be anchored in the ocean behind Rosecliff, transforming the ocean view into the illusion of Newport Harbor.

Yet one of the most memorable stories surrounding Rosecliff involves not Mrs. Oelrichs but Ray Alan Van Clief, who purchased the estate in 1942. Van Clief began extensive renovations—for there had been severe damage due to burst pipes—making all the arrangements by long-distance telephone. When the work was completed, he headed up to Newport to a waiting dinner. Ironically, on the road from Providence, Van Clief was killed in an automobile crash and never stepped foot in the mansion.

The great mansions of Newport—preserved in all their 1930s splendor—are opened today for public tours, and many have served as sets for lavish period films such as *The Great Gatsby* and *The Betsy.*

*LEFT:* Built in 1851–52 for the China Trade merchant William Shepard Wetmore, the monumental granite Château-sur-Mer was the most palatial of the Newport mansions until the Vanderbilts arrived. *Newport, Rhode Island*

*ABOVE:* Several rooms at Château-sur-Mer were remodeled in the 1870s, including the Renaissance Revival–style dining room. Designed by Florentine sculptor Luigi Frullini, the elaborately carved overmantel features a tribute to Bacchus. *Newport, Rhode Island*

## THE VANDERBILT FAMILY LEGACY

The Vanderbilt family was known for building extravagant, palatial homes. One of the oldest of America's wealthy families, the fifty-nine room Fifth Avenue mansion of William Henry Vanderbilt (1821–1896) remains the most elegant residence in Manhattan, while less than one hundred miles north, the Hyde Park mansion of Frederick Vanderbilt is one of the finest Beaux-Arts country houses in the nation.

The Vanderbilt family arrived in America in the mid-seventeenth century and were quickly established as fairly prosperous farmers on New York's Staten Island. It was not until the time of Cornelius Vanderbilt (1794–1877), however, that the family name became synonymous with

*LEFT:* Known as the Gold Room, the ballroom at Marble House boasts the most opulent ornamentation in all of Newport. The wall panels are of carved gilt, and the painted ceiling was inspired by Tintoretto. *Newport, Rhode Island*

extraordinary wealth. Legend has it that at the age of sixteen, with a $100 loan from his mother, Cornelius launched a ferry service across New York Bay. Within a few years, he had established a fleet of over a hundred ships, with routes through much of the Western Hemisphere. Some fifty years later, he became known as the biggest tycoon in the budding American railroad industry.

The large and wealthy family soon established homesteads throughout the Eastern seaboard. The Vanderbilts became the greatest patrons of architect Richard Morris Hunt, who worked almost solely on their homes from the 1880s until his death in 1895. From Hunt's vision and the Vanderbilts' money and taste for fine surroundings, some of the finest homes in North America were born.

The Vanderbilts commissioned Hunt for two mansions in Newport, Rhode Island, the posh resort town that was no stranger to stately homes. In 1888, Hunt began work on Marble House, a

*ABOVE:* Within the formal Italian gardens of Vanderbilt House, a pool is surrounded by pergolas and a classical-style pavilion. *Hyde Park, New York*

*FOLLOWING PAGE:* Marble House, the first of many opulent Vanderbilt houses in Newport, is one of the finest examples of Neoclassicism in America. The façade's four soaring Corinthian columns were based on those of the ancient Temple of the Sun at Heliopolis. *Newport, Rhode Island*

French baroque–style palace, for William K. Vanderbilt and his wife, Alva Smith Vanderbilt. It took four years to build, and was constructed under secrecy, with high walls surrounding the estate to keep out curious eyes. Comprised of over 500,000 cubic feet of marble, and costing an estimated $11,000,000, Marble House was envisioned as a "temple to the arts" in America.

William turned ownership of the estate over to Alva upon its completion in 1892, and spent only two summers there before Alva divorced him in 1895. The daughter of an Alabama cotton broker, Alva Smith is said to have married William for money and position, and was just as shrewd in ensuring that her daughter Consuelo's position was equally secure. Five months after her divorce, she hosted a spectacular coming-out party for Consuelo, and successfully married her off to a British duke who was staying as a guest at Marble House at the time. Consuelo divorced her husband in 1921 to marry for love rather than money. Alva herself married Oliver Hazard Perry Belmont in 1895, and moved to his nearby Belcourt Castle. Marble House remained unoccupied until Belmont's death in 1908, whereupon Alva—by this time a staunch political activist—reopened the estate to raise money for the women's suffrage movement.

*ABOVE:* Architect Richard Morris Hunt modeled Marble House after the Petite Trianon at Versailles. The stone palace utilizes more than 500,000 cubic feet of American, Italian, and African marbles. *Newport, Rhode Island*

*RIGHT:* The Gothic Room at Marble House displays Mrs. Vanderbilt's collection of rare medieval and Renaissance art objects. *Newport, Rhode Island*

*ABOVE:* Kingscote architect Richard Upjohn was a leading practitioner of the Gothic Revival style. The pointed arches and decorative woodwork of the style blended well with Victorian furnishings, as seen in the twin parlors, filled with furnishings accumulated by four generations of the King family, who occupied the house for over one hundred years. *Newport, Rhode Island*

*ABOVE:* Kingscote—now one of the oldest Newport summer houses still remaining—
seems somewhat modest in comparison to the enormous mansions that appeared later.
It was built for Georgia plantation owner George Noble Jones in 1839, at a time when many
well-to-do Southerners spent their summers in the Northeast. *Newport, Rhode Island*

*ABOVE:* The Breakers, a four-story limestone mansion modeled after the
sixteenth-century palaces of Genoa, was designed for Cornelius Vanderbilt by
architect Richard Morris Hunt and built by an international team of artists
and craftsmen. It is now a National Historic Landmark. *Newport, Rhode Island*

The paint was barely dry on Marble House when Hunt began work in 1893 on The Breakers, also in Newport, for Cornelius Vanderbilt. Originally calling for a two-story villa to replace the original Breakers, which had burned down in 1892, the Vanderbilts wound up scrapping Hunt's original plan and demanded something larger and more elaborate. The resulting structure was a huge oceanfront palace, based on those of sixteenth-century Genoa. The mansion is a combination of Hunt's signature beaux-arts style and Cornelius Vanderbilt's personal involvement. Cornelius was the oldest son of William Henry Vanderbilt who, despite his vast, inherited wealth, started out as a bank clerk earning—and believed to have lived on—fifty dollars per month. His work ethic followed him through his life, and he continued working long hours even after becoming chairman of the family railroad empire.

Cornelius is said to have played a crucial role in the planning of The Breakers, determining the final size and shape of the house as well as the interior furnishings. The Breakers features rare marbles, frescoes, sculptures, plasterwork, and mosaics throughout its seventy rooms.

But for both the Vanderbilts and Hunt, the most ambitious project was far from Newport. In a family as well known for building grand homes as it was for amassing great wealth, William's youngest

*BELOW:* Filled with marble, adorned with sculptural elements, and encrusted with gilded bronze, the dining room at The Breakers is the most magnificently appointed in all of this exclusive community. *Newport, Rhode Island*

*ABOVE:* The furnishings and draperies of The Breakers' Music Room are made of red Italian cut velvet. The room was constructed in Paris and shipped to Newport for assembly. *Newport, Rhode Island*

*RIGHT:* The eastern façade of The Breakers faces the sea, and seems to overwhelm its surroundings. The arched double loggia that fills the space between the massive end wings was furnished during warm weather for use as outdoor living space. *Newport, Rhode Island*

son, George Washington Vanderbilt—a quiet and intellectual young man concerned more with culture than commerce—outdid them all with Biltmore House.

The largest and most ambitious home in America, Biltmore House, near Asheville, North Carolina, boasts over four acres of floor space. Vanderbilt challenged architect Hunt and landscape designer Frederick Law Olmstead to create a country estate that would rival the great manors of Europe. From 1889 to 1895, an army of skilled artisans labored on the massive undertaking. Today, Biltmore remains the largest private house ever built in the United States.

Along with its 250 rooms, the mansion features a 780-foot-long façade that seems to assert its size and importance against the backdrop of the surrounding mountains. Inside, the main floor boasts a light-filled garden court surrounded by public rooms in which the Vanderbilts entertained their guests. An imposing Banquet Hall, measuring 72 by 42 feet with a 70-foot-high vaulted ceiling,

*LEFT:* Graceful stone lions guard the entrance to the Biltmore estate. *Asheville, North Carolina*

*ABOVE:* The largest private house ever built in the United States, Biltmore was designed by architect Richard Morris Hunt in the style of the châteaux of the Loire Valley. *Asheville, North Carolina*

*RIGHT:* The immense banquet hall at Biltmore measures 72 by 42 feet and soars to 70 feet in height. Five sixteenth-century Flemish tapestries are displayed around the room. *Asheville, North Carolina*

*BELOW:* Set on a 125,000-acre domain, Biltmore is surrounded by twelve square miles of land. Noted landscape architect Frederick Law Olmsted created naturalistic designs for much of the property. *Asheville, North Carolina*

throughout, with details and furnishings in marble, crystal, silk, and gilt.

Though the Vanderbilts were known for their entertaining, Biltmore was first and foremost a home. George married and raised his only child Cornelia there, and it is on the second floor that the Vanderbilts' private quarters were located. Reflecting the Victorian notion of modesty and decorum, the second-floor rooms—which included the family's living quarters as well as a series of guest rooms—are arranged around a central Living Hall to accommodate socializing and entertaining without invading the sanctity of the bedroom. A lower level hosts—in addition to staff quarters and common rooms, the kitchen, and laundry—an indoor swimming pool and a bowling alley.

Not to be overshadowed by the splendor of the mansion are the equally impressive gardens at Biltmore. The gardens and house are supplied with fresh flowers from the estate's glass-ceilinged conservatory, and the estate's own Biltmore Forest was one of the country's first experiments in reforestation. The grounds also feature an Italian garden, with symmetrical pools, gravel paths, and manicured lawns enclosed by hedges and stone walls. A separate walled garden was originally planned as a kitchen garden, but it became "a garden of ornament rather than utility" at Vanderbilt's insistence. Its grape arbor, fruit trees, and flower beds were designed to produce a unending parade of seasonal color.

became the site of the family's formal entertaining, including birthday parties for their daughter, Cornelia, and annual Christmas parties. A lush billiards room, decorated in dark wood with oriental rugs and heavy leather furnishings, served as the center of a series of rooms that became known as the Bachelor's Wing, the headquarters for all masculine activities in the house. An expansive library housing more than twenty thousand books is set off by itself. The Victorian decor is magnificent

*RIGHT:* Biltmore's library, which houses more than twenty thousand volumes, is dominated by a magnificent eighteenth-century ceiling painting by Pelligrini. *Asheville, North Carolina*

*RIGHT:* Cotton planter Haller Nutt's octagonal Longwood Plantation, also known as Nutt's Folly, was conceived as "a remembrancer of Eastern magnificence which few will judge misplaced as it looms up against the mellowed azure of a Southern sky." *Natchez, Mississippi*

*RIGHT:* Real estate millionaire Henry E. Huntington, also a well-known bibliophile, amassed one of the world's most outstanding private libraries, and his wife, Arabella, was an important art collector. The Huntington estate houses a renowned art museum and library. *San Marino, California*

*LEFT:* **Now a renowned bed and breakfast, Morey Mansion has been called "America's favorite Victorian home."** *Redlands, California*

## OTHER VICTORIAN MANSIONS

Not all the wealthy Americans of the Gilded Age made their fortunes as captains of industry, nor did they all settle down in Newport. And although the Beaux-Arts Movement influenced many designs, the genteel Victorian style pervaded.

One of the finest homes in the Midwest, the David Davis Mansion in Bloomington, Illinois, was completed in 1872 for United States Supreme Court Justice David Davis and his wife, Sarah. Formally named Clover Lawn, Davis's original estate was a working farm, with a carriage barn, foaling shed, stable, and woodhouse which still remain on the property. In 1870 Davis commissioned Alfred Piquenard, one of the region's leading architects, to design the new brick house which would replace the frame farmhouse that the family had occupied for some twenty-eight years. Piquenard designed a home true to the Victorian form, incorporating a diverse array of textures and shapes. Inside, the floor plan reflects the Victorian sense of propriety, with distinct divisions between private family rooms, servants quarters, and visitor areas. Sarah Davis, who described her new home as "comfortable and convenient," was involved in all the decorating, as well as in the planning of the new ornamental flower garden. Fine furnishings reflect Sarah's genteel tastes as well as the Victorian standard of formality.

The Victorian ideal, however, was not always so strictly adhered to. A popular and fairly common building style at the turn of the century, Victorian homes have loaned themselves to countless reinterpretations that range from the subtle blending of styles to more eccentric variations.

*FOLLOWING PAGE:*
**In the late 1880s lumber magnate William Carson commissioned architects Samuel and Joseph C. Newsom to build a prominent Victorian mansion next to his lumberyards.** *Eureka, California*

*LEFT:* The Davis Mansion's public rooms (the parlor and dining room) were divided from the private areas that were reserved for family use, including the well-stocked library. *Bloomington, Illinois*

*ABOVE:* Though not ostentatious, the entry hall of the Davis Mansion is suitably formal, complete with rich wood details and an elaborate ceiling medallion. The central hallway separates the building's public and private rooms. *Bloomington, Illinois*

*RIGHT:* The Davis Mansion features a genteel Victorian interior. Many of the rooms include marble fireplaces, lace curtains, and wall-to-wall carpeting. *Bloomington, Illinois*

*ABOVE:* Constructed for U.S. Supreme Court Justice David Davis, the Davis Mansion (designed by architect Alfred Piquenard) unites elements of several styles into a typically Victorian design. No two pairs of windows are the same, and each of the seven chimneys are different sizes and shapes. *Bloomington, Illinois*

*LEFT:* Sprawling over several acres, the 160-room Winchester Mystery House incorporates many neo-Gothic elements such as turrets, spires, towers, and flying buttresses. *San Jose, California*

## THE STRANGEST VICTORIAN MANSION OF ALL

The story of the estate of Sarah L. Winchester in San Jose, California, remains one of the most intriguing architectural legends in American history. The Winchester Mystery House, a 160-room, $5,500,000 Victorian mansion, was designed and built with no master plan, as directed by the whim of the widow of the rifle manufacturer.

Sarah Winchester met and married William Wirt Winchester during the Civil War. They had one child, who died only a month after birth. Fifteen years later, William died of tuberculosis. Legend has it that the grief-stricken Sarah consulted a medium, who told her that the spirits of all those killed by the rifles manufactured by her family had taken her loved ones as revenge and would continue to haunt her forever. The medium then told her that she could escape the curse—perhaps even achieve eternal life—by purchasing a house in the West and to continually build upon it as the spirits directed.

Sarah moved to what is now San Jose in 1884 and bought an eight-room house. With no real plans and a great deal of money, she kept an army of carpenters, gardeners, and domestic servants busy for the next thirty-eight years. She built impulsively, seemingly by whim. The house sprawled over the surrounding acres, engulfing several outlying buildings as it grew. Inside, a maze of tunnels, trap doors, and staircases without purpose snaked through the structure, some leading to secret passages through the house while others often ended at a brick wall. Windows and doors opened to expose solid walls, and entire rooms were made inaccessible in the constant construction.

*LEFT:* Beginning with an eight-room farmhouse in 1884, Sarah Winchester apparently followed the advice of her spiritualistic medium and continued to add to and remodel her home steadily until her death thirty-eight years later. *San Jose, California*

An intensely private and eccentric person, Sarah Winchester refused to be photographed and did not like to be seen by outsiders or by her servants. Through her intricate, albeit somewhat haphazard, system of tunnels and secret passages, she attempted to take different paths each time she moved through her house, ostensibly to throw off the spirits that were stalking her. During her later years, she would see only her butler, and the only known photograph of her is said to have been snapped by a gardener who took the picture from a hiding place without her knowledge.

Arguments persist over whether Sarah was insane or just extremely eccentric, with the time and financial resources to indulge her somewhat unconventional beliefs. Regardless of her mental state, it is fair to say that Sarah remained haunted, in one way or another, by the legacy of a fortune built on guns and killing. Her eccentric home, now open to the public, is a vivid testament to her state of mind.

*RIGHT:* Not only was the Winchester Mystery House built entirely according to the owner's whim and without a master plan, but many apparently functional features turn out to be useless or arbitrary. *San Jose, California*

*LEFT:* A news photo illustrates the perplexing maze of dead-end passages and stairways that Mrs. Winchester had created in her Mystery House. *San Jose, California*

*RIGHT:* Stairs that lead nowhere and doors opening up onto solid walls are just two devices planned by Mrs. Winchester to confuse the spirits she believed were trying to haunt her. *San Jose, California*

# CHAPTER THREE

# *PALAZZOS*

America's deep South has a long history of luxurious estates, with beautiful Georgian homes built on large, working plantations. But the Gilded Age saw the rise of a new kind of estate in the South, as wealthy merchants bought huge tracts of land and built luxury manors designed not as part of a profit-making estate but as a representation of wealth earned elsewhere.

The warm coastal climates of Florida, Georgia, and the Carolinas made the South a natural choice for wealthy families desiring a palatial vacation home they could use year-round. Inspired by the villas of southern Europe, architects set about creating pleasure palaces that captured the beauty and restful feel of Spain and northern Italy. Combining elements of Renaissance and Gothic architecture, estates such as Ca'd'Zan and Vizcaya are extraordinary examples of craftmanship and vision, with distinctive, whimsical touches.

## CA'D'ZAN

It is said that when John and Mable Ringling, the wealthy owners of the famed circus, approached architect Dwight James Baum with preliminary plans for their Florida estate, the architect went pale. Inspired by a trip to Venice, the Ringlings envisioned an Italianate palace, with elements based on the Doge's Palace and even the towers of

*BELOW:* **All the exterior decorative work on Ca'd'Zan is executed in intricately detailed terra-cotta, considered some of the finest terra-cotta work in the country.** *Sarasota, Florida*

*LEFT:* Ca'd'Zan, the home of John and Mabel Ringling of circus fame, was linitially inspired by Mabel's trip to Venice. The mansion's unusual name is Venetian dialect for "House of John." *Sarasota, Florida*

*RIGHT:* Circus mogul John Ringling of the Ringling Bros. and Barnum & Bailey Circus poses on the grounds of Ca'd'Zan with his German police dog, a gift from Haggenbach, Germany's circus king. *Sarasota, Florida*

*RIGHT:* Circus mogul John Ringling of the Ringling Bros. and Barnum & Bailey Circus poses on the grounds of Ca'd'Zan with his German police dog, a gift from Haggenbach, Germany's circus king. *Sarasota, Florida*

*BELOW:* An aerial view of the red-roofed thirty-one-room Ca'd'Zan clearly shows the immense marble-paved terrace that leads to the dock where Mabel Ringling moored her Venetian gondola and where guests could board John Ringling's yacht. *Sarasota, Florida*

New York's original Madison Square Garden.

The completed Ca'd'Zan ("House of John"), however, is an eclectic marriage of different architectural elements, with minimal references to either the Venetian palace or the Garden. With separate architects for each of the estate's major buildings, the decorative work on the exterior of the Sarasota, Florida, palace is executed almost entirely in terra-cotta, often glazed with brilliant colors personally approved by Mable Ringling. Created by Oram W. Ketchum of Pennsylvania, the terra-cotta work at Ca'd'Zan is considered to be some of the finest in the country.

A mixture of styles and details both grand and whimsical work together on this structure. The west façade on Sarasota Bay features a fantastic marble terrace, incorporating a distinctive geometric design that gives the palace an assertive beauty even when viewed from a long distance. From the terrace, steps lead out to the dock where John's yacht and Mable's gondola—which she imported from Venice—awaited. Sixteenth-century Spanish tiles cover the roofs, and a Turkish-style open kiosk tower offers a view of the bay and surrounding islands. Twelve-foot-high carved walnut doors mark the main entrance, which is approached from a circular drive.

Inside the thirty-one room house, details large and small attest to the Ringlings' personal involvement in the construction and decoration of the estate. In one room, the entire bar of glass of the Cicardi Winter Palace restaurant in St. Louis is reconstructed. It was said that John Ringling liked the place so much, he bought it and brought it home.

A huge central living room features a skylight of colored glass, framed by a cypress ceiling decorated with paintings of mythological figures and the signs of the zodiac. A huge crystal chandelier, which originally hung in New York's Waldorf-Astoria hotel, is suspended from the center. An Aeolian organ is situated on one wall. With four thousand pipes hidden behind tapestries on the balcony above, the organ can be played manually or electrically. Ringling had an expert from New York build the organ on-site, at a cost of $50,000. The same expert constructed a similar organ on the nearby estate of John's brother, Charles Ringling.

Through the years, the Ringlings filled their many guest rooms with prominent industrialists, celebrities, and politicians of the era, entertaining in high style in the home they built for fun and pleasure. They also built a large and elaborate art museum alongside the mansion, both of which were bequeathed to the people of Florida upon John's death. The Ringling mansion remains a unique marriage of the artisans' expertise and the owners' fantasy.

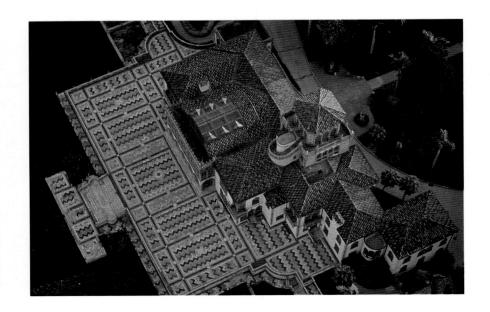

*LEFT:* Soaring Gothic-arched windows frame a checkerboard floor composed of black Belgian marble and white Alabama marble in Sarasota's Ca'd'Zan. *Sarasota, Florida*

*LEFT:* The train car known as "Rambler" was built for Flagler's personal use. The exterior bears the official colors of the Florida East Coast Railway, and the oak paneling inside includes carvings of Flagler's monogram. *Palm Beach, Florida*

*BELOW:* The large interior courtyard of Whitehall was inspired by a Spanish Colonial dwelling Flagler had seen in Havana. *Palm Beach, Florida*

## WHITEHALL

Despite its palatial splendor, Whitehall represented homeyness to its owner, Florida developer Henry Morrison Flagler. "That was what I wanted, a home," Flagler said of his Palm Beach marble palace, which was constructed around an inner courtyard filled with lush greenery.

Flagler (1830–1913) was a partner of John D. Rockefeller in the founding of Standard Oil Company, one of the biggest of the big-business trusts. When Flagler's first wife died in 1881 he left the oil business; two years later he remarried, and he and his bride honeymooned in Florida, which introduced Flagler to the state's development possibilities. He built numerous hotels and resorts and established a railroad from Jacksonville to Key West. By the end of his life he had managed to develop Florida's entire east coast, establishing Miami, Palm Beach, Daytona, and St. Augustine as famous resorts.

When Flagler married for the third time, in 1901, at the age of seventy-one, his new bride was thirty-seven years younger. It was for this woman, Mary Lily Kenan, that Flagler built Whitehall. In 1903 the house was officially opened with a grand masquerade ball.

The architects of Whitehall were John Merven Carrère and Thomas Hastings, who met while attending the Ecole des Beaux-Arts in Paris in the 1880s. Both descended from wealthy families themselves, their connections enabled them to secure very prominent commissions. Their first design for Flagler was the elaborate Ponce de Leon Hotel in St. Augustine. Billed as "the world's finest hotel," the Ponce de Leon was the first of the great hotels intended to bring vacationers to Florida. Like the Ponce de Leon, Whitehall was originally designed in a Spanish Renaissance style, but as construction progressed Flagler decided he preferred "something more on the Colonial order." The only Spanish features

ultimately used at Whitehall were the interior courtyard and red-tiled roof.

In 1925, Flagler's heirs sold Whitehall, which then served as a luxury hotel until 1959. Restored by Flagler's granddaughter, the structure became the Flagler Museum in 1960. The carefully refurbished rooms have been returned to their original splendor. Filled with many of the original furnishings and with family memorabilia, Whitehall today offers an inspired glimpse into the opulent life of its heyday.

*BELOW:* **A wide entrance walk leads to the stately façade of Whitehall. The fluted columns are flanked by massive white marble urns.** *Palm Beach, Florida*

## VIZCAYA

Situated on southeast Florida's Biscayne Bay, the Villa Vizcaya derives its name from Spain's Vizcaya province on the Bay of Biscay. The building was first envisioned as a Spanish house, but the design gradually took on more Italianate influences and was modeled on the 1670 Venetian baroque Villa Rezzonico.

Vizcaya was built for James Deering, son of the founder of Deering Harvester Company. In 1902 the Deerings merged with another company to become the International Harvester Company, at that time the country's largest manufacturer of farm machinery. James studied art and apparently hoped to become a painter but was instead made vice president of the company. He retired a multi-millionaire in 1910 and chose Florida as his winter residence. He determined to amass an art collection and to build a house dedicated to art.

The man ultimately in charge of the project was Paul Chalfin. Originally hired as an art consultant, Chalfin eventually became the guiding force behind it all, overseeing architect F. Burrall Hoffman, Jr., and landscape architect Diego Suarez, who created the estate's formal gardens.

Each of the four sides of the villa embody different architectural modes marching through four centuries. The façade that faces the bay is built in fifteenth-century style, while the north-facing side resembles sixteenth-century mannerism. On the south, facing the gardens, is the seventeenth-century grandeur of Louis XIV, and the entrance façade evokes the eighteenth century.

The villa was laid out around a courtyard scheme, with the major formal rooms proceeding

*FOLLOWING PAGE:* Ca'd'Zan's central tower is an open kiosk built in the Turkish style. Reached by an open stairway, the tower boasts a spectacular view of Sarasota Bay and the barrier islands. *Sarasota, Florida*

*LEFT:* The secret garden is just one of the surprises prepared for a visitor to Vizcaya. Others include a waterside gazebo and an outdoor casino. *Miami, Florida*

*RIGHT:* Inspired by Italian designs, the gardens of Vizcaya incorporate sculpture, fountains, and architectural elements to create an array of expansive vistas and charming walkways. *Miami, Florida*

*LEFT:* Designer Paul Chalfin declared that at Vizcaya he had created something "up to now unachieved in the new world . . . a house and garden that date from a proud and vigorous past." *Miami, Florida*

around it. Rather than reproducing any particular historical building, Vizcaya combined the styles of several countries and various eras into an art historical collage. Each room offered a different flavor, from the Renaissance Hall to the Marie Antoinette Salon to the Robert Adam Room to the Rococo Room. The whole was filled with rich fabrics, imported building materials, and antiquities collected in Europe.

Though the building was not entirely completed until 1921, Vizcaya officially opened on Christmas 1916, with a marvelous pageant designed by Chalfin. Deering arrived by yacht, as the building's lights winked on in sequence and cannons blew a salute. The evening was topped off with a masquerade ball. For the last few years of his life, Deering continued to enjoy winters at Vizcaya, arriving in December and staying through April, in the home that one newspaper called "The Grandest House in America."

*ABOVE:* Multimillionaire James Deering and his designer, Paul Chalfin, incorporated numerous Italianate influences into the imposing structure of Vizcaya. The immense boat-shaped stone barge resulted from the need to disguise a small island that had been formed by dredging operations. *Miami, Florida*

*RIGHT:* Many of the architectural elements, furnishings, and fabrics for Vizcaya were imported from around the world. Much of the interior was designed to display Deering's collection of decorative objects. *Miami, Florida*

## SWAN HOUSE

Luxury living in the South was not limited to the resort homes of Florida. After the Civil War, much of Atlanta, Georgia, was left in ruins. The area was ripe with opportunity for growth during the Gilded Age, and many fine homes were built then. The Swan House, completed in 1928 for Edward Hamilton Inman and his wife Emily, stands out as an exquisite example of 1920s Atlanta residential architecture.

Inman's family had settled in Atlanta just after the Civil War and made a fortune as cotton brokers. Raised in Atlanta and educated at Princeton, Inman was a prominent member of Atlanta society, serving as city councilman and in 1918 running unsuccessfully for mayor. He was one of the first men in the city to own an automobile, and he became an avid auto racer, winning the Atlanta Journal Cup in 1908.

Designed by Atlanta architect Philip Trammel Shutze and named for the swan motif found throughout the interior, the Swan House combines influences with a decidedly Tuscan feel. A baroque garden façade incorporates a cascade fountain inspired by one the Inmans had seen at an Italian villa, flanked by stairs that lead from the lawn to the house. The main entrance includes a heavily framed doorway surrounded with attractive ornamentation. This doorway is flanked by arched wall niches, each inset with a shell motif and colored with tinted stucco. Throughout the building, the architect used tinted stucco in sienna and yellow, graduating the color to give the walls the weathered appearance of an old Italian villa.

In 1966, the Atlanta History Society purchased the estate and most of its furnishings, and in 1982 the architect Shutze bequeathed his own formidable collection of decorative artifacts along with his research library to the society. Today, the Swan House is a public museum, a testament to the distinctive style of 1930s Atlanta.

*ABOVE:* **Completed in 1928, Swan House was designed by architect Philip Trammel Shutze. The elegant baroque façade of the garden entrance is topped with a pedimented attic gable pierced with a bull's-eye window.** *Atlanta, Georgia*

*LEFT:* **Cherubs cavort with a dolphin in a fountain on the grounds of Swan House. The site features numerous examples of statuary and other garden architecture.** *Atlanta, Georgia*

# AFTERWORD

## THE END OF AN ERA

The Gilded Age ended abruptly with the Stock Market crash 1929, but in truth it had been dying long before many of the great homes were constructed. The Sherman Anti-Trust Act of 1890 put an end to the great monopolies, and would-be

*ABOVE:* The graceful Italianate structure of Evergreen House sits amid twenty-six wooded acres. The house was the residence of ambassador John Work Garrett and his wife, Alice Warder Garrett. *Baltimore, Maryland*

tycoons of the future were left to seek their fortunes in a more competitive environment. And while the major fortunes won during the age of the Trust continued to flourish through the Roaring Twenties, and most surviving the Great Depression as well, the boundless optimism of the Gilded Age was gone.

Socially, too, the wealthy class had lost its luster by the turn of the century. The very wealthy, once regarded as heroes of sorts, had been exposed as robber barons, and the working class was no longer easily impressed by their money or stature. Additionally, the immoral behavior

enjoyed by many among the wealthy—vividly exposed in newspapers such as Hearst's—led to a general distaste for the moneyed class. Perhaps most telling are the events surrounding the murder of the renowned architect Stanford White in 1906.

White, who had designed many of the great mansions of Newport and elsewhere and who was himself was one of the most celebrated figures of the Gilded Age, was murdered on the roof of Madison Square Garden by the jealous husband of his ex-lover. The murderer, the wealthy and eccentric playboy Harry K. Thaw (who was rumored to have lit his cigars with five-dollar bills), was tried in what was at the time considered to be the trial of the century. Lewd and shocking details about White and other members of society's upper crust were revealed in painstaking detail by New York's twenty-six daily newspapers. The story was seen as exemplary of the degeneracy of the upper class. The golden boys of the age had, in these few moments, become forever tarnished.

Yet the homes of the Gilded Age remain in all their palatial splendor. Most have been preserved and are today open to the public as museums of fine art and culture. They tell the fascinating story of a time unparalleled in American history, when the entire nation believed that anyone could become wealthy with determination, hard work, and a little luck.

*RIGHT:* Vizcaya's formal gardens cover ten acres and feature only plants native to the region. *Miami, Florida*

# INDEX

Page numbers in **bold-face** type indicate photo captions.